MARIA WEBER

Your Dog Does Not Speak English

First published by Trunk Up Books 2025

Copyright © 2025 by Maria Weber

All rights reserved. No part of this publication may be reproduced, stored or transmitted in any form or by any means, electronic, mechanical, photocopying, recording, scanning, or otherwise without written permission from the publisher. It is illegal to copy this book, post it to a website, or distribute it by any other means without permission.

First edition

ISBN: 978-1-958368-10-7

*This book was professionally typeset on Reedsy.
Find out more at reedsy.com*

My husband, Jerry Weber, puts up with my dog obsession.

Contents

Acknowledgments	ii
What to Expect	iv
1 Greetings Gone Bad	1
2 Kids and Canines	7
3 Doggy Discipline	16
4 Feeding Your Furry Friend	38
5 Tall Tails: Myths About Dogs & Their Behavior	43
6 It all starts with you	51

Acknowledgments

I have been blessed to have been able to work with so many talented trainers throughout the years. It took a lot of work and patience to take me from a newbie that knew only what I had picked up from TV, movies and common beliefs to someone who is helping spread the joy of responsible dog ownership and dog sports with others. I want to take a moment and thank all those who helped me along my journey.

My obedience trainers from puppy all the way to competition obedience and rally:

- Karol Mitcheff
- Briget Kilcommon
- Sandy Heimberg
- Joni Monnich
- Don Shiffer
- Fred Buroff
- My agility and nose work trainers:
- Rochelle Tonelli
- Missy Bortel

My fellow Siberian Husky owners who taught me by example that our stubborn and independent breed could compete alongside the more traditional breeds:

- Dr Lee Cera
- Jennifer Seul
- Noel Dagley
- Theresa Przybylski
- Randy Johnson

And finally, everyone at Stone City Kennel Club in New Lenox, IL and K9 Tailshakers in Frankfort, IL for offering such wonderful and knowledgeable trainers.

What to Expect

Twelve years ago, my life changed when an eight-week old Siberian husky puppy joined my family. Over all the excitement, it was hard to imagine just how unprepared we were!

I have always loved dogs. I spent time around various family member's dogs and enjoyed interacting with them or just watching their antics. When we brought Comet home, I thought I was prepared. I was 46 years old at the time and knew a thing or two about dogs.

Boy, was I wrong.

We were in way over our heads. I needed help, and a lot of it if we were going to survive with our house and our sanity intact.

I was lucky to have several great training options in my area, but even after the puppy classes, I still had a high-energy nut on my hands. I had just as much to learn as my new puppy. This led me to a whole new world of dog sports that I never knew existed.

Before I knew it, and with a lot of encouragement from various instructors, Comet and I were entering dog trials and competitions. I never imagined myself competing in any kind of dog event—not in my wildest dreams! But one thing led to another, and we became a successful team. Over the last decade she has earned titles in Agility, Obedience, Rally Obedience, Scent Work, and many more in addition to being a working therapy dog at our local hospital and assisted living facilities.

Comet was the first Siberian husky in the American Kennel

Club's (AKC) history to earn the Rally Obedience Championship Title, Rally Master 2, 3, 4 and 5. She was also the first Siberian Husky to earn the AKC Performer Elite title which is also referred to as Freestyle Agility (Dancing with your dog).

In the past decade I have become a therapy dog evaluator and conduct therapy dog workshops. I teach rally obedience classes and run a free youth training club for kids 8–17 years old where I teach basic obedience, agility, and scent work. I am also an AKC evaluator for the Canine Good Citizen (CGC), Temperament Test (ATT) and Agility's Course Ability Test (ACT).

If you're looking to understand your pet better and take a step in the right direction, you've picked up the right book. Over the years, I've come across countless myths and misconceptions about dogs—some that I once believed myself and others that I've frequently seen in fellow dog owners. While some of these misunderstandings might seem harmless, others can lead to serious issues, even putting your dog's safety at risk. In this book, I'll address these common myths and offer practical tips that can make a real difference in your relationship with your dog. By clearing up these misconceptions, you'll not only gain a deeper understanding of your canine companion but also create a more harmonious, happy life together.

1

Greetings Gone Bad

Your dog is an animal. Yes, they are a loving member of your family, but they are still an animal trying to live by human rules that probably seem ridiculous in their eyes. *What we see as a friendly gesture, your dog may interpret as a threat.*

As pet owners, we often unknowingly put our dogs in a position where they feel they must lash out or defend themselves. Actions that seem harmless to humans, such as petting a dog when first meeting them, can be stressful for some dogs. If that fear or stress is strong enough, it could result in a bite.

Too often, I've heard "it came out of nowhere!" when a person speaks about a dog bite, but truly, the signs were there and it is our responsibility as the dog's owner to be the dog's advocate. The average person genuinely believes they are interacting correctly with your dog when in reality they may be causing your dog considerable stress.

Making yourself familiar with basic canine body language to recognize signs such as stress and fear. Learning basic canine etiquette will go a long way towards your dog's happiness.

What NOT to do when greeting a dog

Do not offer your hand for a dog to sniff

When you meet a dog for the first time, most people put out a hand and let the dog sniff their fingers. It's a great way to warm them up to you, right? WRONG! This is actually an excellent way to get bit.

This action is so commonplace that I still occasionally catch myself doing it—and I know better now! Most dogs will tolerate your fingers, but to some dogs this can be seen as aggression. It just takes once for a dog to misinterpret your well-intended greeting.

If you're thinking to yourself, "I've been doing this my whole life and I still have all my fingers!" here's some advice:

- Don't stick your hand in a blender, even if it's unplugged. The blades are still sharp.
- Don't play with a wood saw, even if it's currently off. All it takes is an on switch.
- Don't stick your fingers in a fan, even if the blades look like they're moving slowly. Your wounds will not agree.
- Don't stick your hands in a strange dog's face, even if it looks calm or friendly. For their sake and yours.

Don't scratch a dog's ears or head

If your hand survives being offered up as a sacrifice, the next common way to greet an unfamiliar dog is to scratch its head, often between the ears. The problem is that a nervous dog will see you as a stranger coming at their face and if they feel threatened or fearful enough, their instincts may take over.

If you already have a familiar relationship with a dog, these scratches are canine bliss! But for a dog that doesn't have reason to trust you, this can be scary.

Don't make direct eye contact

When we meet a new dog it is our natural instinct as a human to look straight into the dog's eyes. Now, dogs you already have a bond with might not mind when you do this. When you hold eye contact with your own dog you usually are gifted with a look of total adoration and love. But we are not talking about a dog that you already have a relationship with here. We are talking about a dog you are meeting for the first time or one you may casually know.

When two dogs have a fixed stare into each other's eyes it is an instinctual way they establish dominance between them. It's like an intense staring contest to see who will concede. Dog to dog eye contact can easily escalate, so if I see it happen between two dogs in one of my classes—especially if their bodies are motionless—I disrupt their view and get distance between them. So, how does this translate into a human to dog interaction?

Staring straight into an unfamiliar dog's eye can be mistaken as aggressive and threatening rather than friendly.

I happen to have two blue eyed dogs, which strangers find fascinating. People often make eye contact with my dogs and they tolerate it, but I invested time and energy into training them. As puppies I rewarded them for eye contact by offering treats when they interacted with strangers in a positive manner. I would sometimes give the stranger the treat to offer the puppy. They learned that new humans equaled a positive experience.

I'm sure they considered that person as having terrible manners for looking straight into their eyes but they learned to expect it.

But a dog accepting an action doesn't mean they enjoy it, and not all dogs come with a naturally trusting demeanor. Just like people, dogs have diverse life experiences that influence how they react. If you catch yourself making eye contact with an unfamiliar dog, work on breaking the habit.

Don't grab the dog's face

Another well-intended but concerning practice is cupping a dog's face in your hands. Imagine that a stranger twice your size approaches you and before you can react, they pull your face to theirs and hold it there between their hands. They stare into your eyes to intimidate you and you can't easily pull away. You feel trapped. What would you do next?

If this was a human-to-human interaction, it would still be threatening. Well, a dog isn't comfortable with it either.

Every part of this situation is aggressive and threatening from the dog's point of view. Their head is restrained and the person looms over them while making eye contact. If the dog lashes out in defense, your face is the likely target.

Let's talk about what to do instead.

Greetings Done Right

First of all—and I cannot stress this enough—you do not need to greet every dog you encounter, nor should you expect your dog to greet every person they meet. Your dog is a thinking, breathing individual with a unique personality. Just like people, not every dog is naturally sociable. Your dog should have the right to choose whether or not they want to greet someone, and they should always have the option to say "no."

For dogs, greeting someone usually involves physical contact. Even the friendliest dogs may not want to interact every time. Give your dog the freedom to choose by learning to read their body language and following their lead. I'll explain more about that in a moment.

How to approach a dog

The first thing you should always do is ask the owner for permission to approach. If they say no, respect their answer without taking offense. You don't know the dog's background—they could be in training, not feeling well, or simply uncomfortable with strangers. The dog might also be protective of their owner, or the owner may just not want to engage. Regardless, their response should guide your actions.

Once you've gotten the go-ahead from the owner, it's time to ask the dog. Yes, you read that correctly—you're going to ask the dog with your actions, and they'll respond with theirs.

Stand a few feet away, within the dog's reach but not intruding on their space. Position yourself at a slight angle rather than facing the dog directly, as this is less intimidating. Eye contact can feel threatening to some dogs, so avoid making direct eye contact. Then, wait and observe.

If the dog *doesn't* move toward you, take it as their polite way of saying they don't want to meet you. End the interaction there. You can still chat with the owner, but ignore the dog entirely.

If the dog *does* approach you, let them take the lead. Allow them a few seconds to sniff you and get comfortable with your scent. While they're doing this, remain at a slight angle. When the dog seems relaxed, gently reach down to pet their side—never their head or face.

Think about how dogs greet each other: they often stand side by side, facing opposite directions. Mimicking this behavior by petting the dog's side is non-threatening and helps them feel at ease. A happy, comfortable dog will usually have a loose, wiggly body, and their tail may wag in a relaxed manner.

Above all, let the dog set the pace. If they back away, give them space. If they stay close or return after stepping back, it's a sign they're comfortable continuing the interaction. Congratulations—you've just made a new friend!

When it comes to greeting dogs, patience and respect go a long way. Dogs, like people, have their own boundaries, preferences, and moods. By learning to interpret their body language and giving them the choice to engage, you help create a safe and positive environment for everyone involved.

Remember, not every dog wants or needs to interact with you—or your dog. And that's okay! Respecting a dog's individuality and their owner's decisions is just as important as any other part of being a responsible pet owner or animal lover.

2

Kids and Canines

Children and dogs often share a natural draw to one another, leading to moments of laughter, play, and exploration. With healthy boundaries, their bond can become a source of joy, love, and growth for both kids and canines alike. In this chapter, we'll explore how to create safe, positive, and engaging interactions that enrich the lives of both your child and your dog.

Do Not Mistake the Dog's Tolerance for Enjoyment

The internet is an endless source of cringe-worthy photos and videos. The most upsetting to me are the pictures of dogs putting up with a child's shenanigans. In these scenarios, either the child has done something independently, or—worse, in my opinion—the parents have arranged the situation just for a photo op. Such situations pose a risk to both the child, who could suffer long-term harm from a bite, and the dog would likely be put down.

When a dog bite occurs, I often hear "it came out of nowhere."

The family insist the child and dog have been the best of friends until the dog suddenly went rogue one day. This is almost certainly not true —most people just don't know the signs or misinterpret them.

It is important to teach your child the proper way to behave around dogs, but you also need to educate yourself on what to watch for. It is also equally important that we, as the dog's guardians, act as the dog's advocate. If a child (or really, anyone) is making your dog uncomfortable it is our job to speak for them. We must get our dogs out of situations that can turn ugly.

Your Dog is Asking for Help

In typical videos showing children interacting with dogs, I often see the dog signaling distress, while the humans misinterpret these signals. A common scenario involves the child dressing the dog up or applying makeup, which the parent perceives as a cute moment between the child and their furry friend. However, my experience suggests something different. In one word, what I'm seeing is "STRESS."

Some signs of stress look like:

- The dog stands eerily still.
- The dog's mouth is tightly closed and tense.
- The dog's eyes are wide open. You may even see the white of their eyes (also called whale eyes or half-moon eyes).
- The dog yawns or scratches excessively when the child plays with them.

But sometimes, it's avoidance. The dog will sometimes look straight at the adult and then look away or the dog may try to simply walk away to get his message across, but the child follows him.

There are many signs that a dog is unhappy or under stress that most humans simply do not recognize as canine communication. Yawning, drooling, excessive licking, tensing, position of ears, look of their eyes, shaking, scratching, walking away, and many more can all be ways your dog is trying to communicate with you. Dogs use the tools available to them which is primarily their body language.

Teach your children to always ask permission before greeting a dog. Kids tend to run right up to a dog and start interacting with him. Even the best of dogs can get startled.

A stranger once approached me at a crowded farmer's market and shoved her 6-month-old baby directly into my Siberian husky's face. My dog is extremely tolerant of children, but the mother would have had no way of knowing that. My dog could have easily reacted to having an object thrust into her face. I quickly got between the child and the dog, which offended the woman. She said she wanted the baby to see the pretty dog. To this day, I'm grateful things didn't turn out differently.

Children must accept that dogs are thinking, breathing creatures and may not want to be their friend. It is perfectly okay to admire that gorgeous dog from a distance.

Don't Ride Your Dog

I've seen countless photos of children riding dogs as if they were horses. It's no wonder that many people think this is not only okay but also cute. But let's be clear: a dog is not a horse. This might seem obvious, yet I still see it happen. **This needs to stop.** People often say, 'The dog likes it. He stands perfectly still to let Junior climb on.' However, a dog standing perfectly still can actually be a red flag.

- **A dog that stands perfectly still may be highly stressed**: This stillness often indicates the dog feels trapped or uncomfortable.
- **Stillness can be a warning**: Before a dog lashes out or bites, he might freeze in place as a final warning.
- **Your dog's tolerance isn't the same as enjoyment**: Just because your dog isn't moving doesn't mean he's happy. He's likely trying to communicate discomfort in the only way he knows how.

Beyond the behavioral signs, there are also physical risks involved:

- **Dogs aren't built to carry weight on their spines**: No matter the dog's size or the child's weight, this can cause pain and injury.
- **Riding can lead to serious physical harm**: A dog that's ridden can strain their neck or spine. Even dogs bred for pulling heavy loads use the muscles in their chest, back, and hindquarters together to pull something behind them, not to carry weight on top of them.

Remember, just because your dog seems to tolerate something doesn't mean it's safe or healthy for him.

Hugs

Humans love hugs. Most of us enjoy giving and receiving them, and we often encourage our kids to hug everyone who visits, so it's no surprise that children also want to hug dogs. But while many dogs will *tolerate* hugs, it doesn't mean they like them. In fact, a hug can make a dog feel trapped.

My older dog, Comet, is a therapy dog at the local hospital and frequently interacts with kids. Many of these children immediately want to hug her, and she'll look up at me with a pleading expression. This is where I advocate for my dog.

- **For older children**, I use the moment as a learning opportunity. I explain what dogs prefer, making sure to stay upbeat and positive. This approach keeps the child enthusiastic about making their new doggy friend happy, while subtly teaching them how to interact appropriately.
- **For younger children or individuals with certain challenges**, I redirect their attention. I might distract them with comments like, "Look at her pretty tail. Isn't it fluffy?" For my Siberian Huskies, I might say, "They love the snow! Look how thick their fur is. Do you think they enjoy winter?" This positive redirection helps keep the child engaged without making them or the dog uncomfortable.

My main goal is to always advocate for my dog, ensuring she isn't placed in a situation that causes her undue stress or discomfort. This is for my dog's safety as well as the child's.

"But He Was Wagging His Tail"

We often think a wagging tail always means a happy dog, but that's not always the case. While a wagging tail *can* indicate happiness, it can also signal fear, stress, submission, or other emotions. A common misunderstanding occurs when people say, 'But he was wagging his tail' after their dog has bitten someone. The tail wagging may have been a sign that the dog was feeling threatened and trying to communicate 'back off,' which was ignored or misunderstood.

Tail communication can vary by breed, so it's important to understand the nuances of your dog's specific breed. For now, let's look at some common tail positions:

- **Happy Tail:** The ideal happy tail is upright and gently swaying back and forth. If your dog is extremely excited, the tail might wag rapidly, and his rear end may shake along with it.
- **Aggressive Tail:** Be cautious of a dog wagging his tail stiffly or held high. This can indicate aggression rather than friendliness.
- **Fearful Tail:** A frightened dog often tucks his tail between his legs. This is a well-known metaphor for fear, as in the phrase 'tuck tail and run.' A tucked tail can also indicate submission, and sometimes a dog may show both behaviors—wagging while his tail is tucked.

Videos of 'guilty' dogs often show signs of fear or nervousness rather than true guilt. It's important to teach children to respect a dog's signals of anxiety and to give the dog space when he shows these signs.

Let Sleeping Dogs Lie

Young children, even toddlers, often want to cuddle with a sleeping dog, and many parents think it's adorable—'Look how much she loves her dog' or 'He sees the dog as a big stuffed animal.' But it's important to step in before the dog gets startled and potentially reacts in a way that could lead to trouble.

This is especially true for older dogs who might have stiff or sore joints. If a dog is suddenly disturbed, they might react defensively if they're in pain or feeling threatened. This could lead to a bite or other issues, and unfortunately, it might result in the dog being rehomed rather than correcting the child's behavior.

Similarly, don't let your children bother a dog while it's eating. I once heard about a parent who proudly showed off their dog's training by letting their child take a treat from the dog's mouth. This kind of thing can be risky and might provoke the dog to react defensively. Remember, it only takes one time for someone to get hurt.

I've had a similar experience myself: At a family gathering, I gave my dog a big bone to enjoy while we ate. When my dad briefly took the bone away to check it out, the dog growled—something I didn't expect from a dog known for being well-behaved. This taught me that even well-trained dogs can react unpredictably if they feel their resources are threatened.

Dogs have their own instincts and boundaries, and no matter how well-trained they are, they can still react unexpectedly if they're startled or annoyed. To keep things safe and happy, it's important to teach kids to respect a dog's space, especially when the dog is resting or eating. This helps prevent misunderstandings and keeps both your child and your dog safe and comfortable.

That Dog is Not a Babysitter

Children playing with their dogs can seem like a scene from a Norman Rockwell painting. It's wonderful when our dogs become one of our child's best friends through childhood, as long as the play is appropriate and supervised.

Here are some key points to remember:

- **Never leave young children unsupervised with the family dog.** Young children, especially toddlers, don't always have the same reasoning as adults. They might act out when frustrated or upset, and this can sometimes be directed at the dog. For example, I recently saw a two-year-old kick a dog simply to move it out of the way. The child wasn't being mean; they just didn't have a better way to express their needs. Most dogs are incredibly patient with kids, but there might come a day when a dog's tolerance runs out.
- **Avoid relying on your dog as a "nanny."** Some people mistakenly assume that their dog will not only keep an eye on the child but also entertain them and alert the parent if something goes wrong. This can be a dangerous assumption.
- **Even the most trustworthy dogs can have a moment of reaction.** Our dogs are tolerant and loving family members who enjoy playing with kids.

However, it only takes one time for things to go wrong.

- One time for the dog to react unexpectedly.
- One time for the child to be bitten or emotionally traumatized.
- One time for the dog to face serious consequences.
- One time for the dog to potentially lose its home or its life.

Always supervise interactions between children and dogs to ensure a safe and happy environment for both.

3

Doggy Discipline

Training your dog is about shaping behaviors, understanding your dog's needs, and reinforcing positive habits. In this chapter, we'll explore training methods that not only foster obedience but also enhance the loving bond between you and your pup. Let's discover how a little patience and consistency can lead to a lifetime of happiness and cooperation.

Emotions & Motivation

We love our dogs and often think of them as members of the family, which is exactly as it should be. But where many people go wrong is forgetting that dogs aren't humans—they don't share the same emotions, motivations, or thought processes we do. It's easy to assume that our dogs think the way we do, but this can lead to big misunderstandings.

There's even a word for this: anthropomorphism, which means attributing human emotions and behaviors to animals. It's something we've all done at one point or another when dealing with our dogs. While it's natural, recognizing that dogs experience the world differently is an important step toward understanding and communicating with them more effectively.

Yes, dogs do share many feelings with us. They have many of the same basic emotions we have such as happiness, fear, loneliness, aggravation, anger, and sadness. There are many emotions that dogs, however, *do not* experience despite some people's insistence; shame, pride, embarrassment, guilt, and spite are among those.

How often do we see pictures of "guilty" looking dogs on the internet, paired with funny captions about their supposed sense of shame? I always feel bad for those dogs—not because they're actually feeling shame (they're not) but because what their humans interpret as guilt is more likely fear, sadness, or appeasement.

I hear it all the time: "My dog feels so guilty when he has an accident in the house," or, "He knows he did something wrong when he chews things up—just look at him!" Many people assume their dog understands exactly what they did wrong based on how they behave when confronted.

But the truth is, dogs don't feel guilt like we do. They live completely in the moment. If you catch your dog with the remote control in his mouth, he probably knows that's what made you upset. But if he chewed it up two hours ago, he has no clue why you're angry now. That "guilty" look? It's not guilt—it's your dog responding to your tone, body language, and emotions right then and there.

Dogs are masters at reading human body language and are sensitive to our emotions. They've developed these skills over time to better adapt to life in the human world. When we come home to a mess—like a potty accident or a chewed-up remote—

and react with anger, our dog's "guilty" behavior isn't about what they did. It's a response to *our actions and emotions* in that moment, not their own.

Most people struggle to believe this at first. They've seen their dog's reaction when they come home to a mess, and it looks like guilt to them. But a simple five-minute experiment usually changes their perspective. Take your dog into a room where he hasn't done anything wrong and is normally allowed to be. Pretend you've caught him in the act of doing something destructive. You might put your hands on your hips, shake a finger at him, and yell, "What did you do?" in an angry tone.

What happens next? Your dog will likely react in a way that looks, to a human, like guilt. But the truth is, he hasn't done anything wrong—he's responding to your actions, not his own behavior. Guilt simply isn't a concept dogs understand. What's really happening is that humans interpret a dog's reaction through the lens of human emotions. Meanwhile, the poor dog is utterly confused. He doesn't understand why you're angry; he only knows that you're upset with him.

Another one I hear all the time is, "My dog is so spiteful!" But dogs aren't spiteful. What's really happening is the owner is connecting two unrelated events that have nothing to do with each other.

If you're gone for a long time and your dog gets into something he shouldn't, it's not because he's trying to get even with you. He's bored—and he probably misses you too. That shoe left on the floor? It not only feels great to chew but also smells like his favorite human, making it irresistible.

This kind of misunderstanding often comes up with house training too. Take the common scenario where someone punishes their dog for going to the bathroom in the house, maybe even rubbing their nose in it. Then the next time the dog needs to go, they do it in the bedroom, and the owner assumes it's out of spite. But it's not spite—it's confusion or even fear caused by the earlier punishment. Dogs just don't think that way.

When we misinterpret our dog's behavior, we often confuse them—and sometimes even make the situation worse. Reacting in a way that instills fear can damage the trust your dog has in you. The last thing you want is for your dog to learn that their human is unpredictable or prone to irrational anger. That kind of relationship isn't stable and certainly isn't what you want to build with your dog.

Inevitable Accidents

Whether you are house-training a new puppy, an older dog that you adopted, or the dog you've had for years, the occasional accident is bound to happen. This is something you must accept as a dog owner and learn the best way to handle the situation without traumatizing your dog.

Many of us grew up believing that rubbing a dog's nose in an accident or dragging them to the spot and scolding them with a rolled-up newspaper was the right way to handle house-training mishaps. These methods, however, are not only ineffective but can actually hinder your training efforts and, in some cases, create even bigger problems.

I once worked with a 3-year-old Australian Shepherd named Macie. Her owner was baffled because Macie, who was completely house-trained, had suddenly started peeing in the house. What began as an isolated incident quickly escalated into a recurring issue, leaving her owner frustrated and confused.

As Macie's trainer, I could immediately picture what might have been happening in their home. When I shared my thoughts, her owner seemed skeptical, so I invited another instructor to weigh in. Without hesitation, they came to the same conclusion I had. It was a classic case of misunderstanding between dog and owner, and the root cause wasn't what Macie's owner expected.

If your house-trained dog suddenly starts having accidents out of the blue, the first step is to take them to the veterinarian as soon as possible. Sudden accidents are often a sign of a medical issue, such as a urinary tract infection, that may be making it difficult for your dog to control their bladder or bowels.

Instead of addressing the root cause, Macie was punished for having an accident in the house by rubbing her nose in the spot she peed in. This completely backfired because Macie did not understand what she was being punished for. As a result, Macie became fearful and started finding more creative, hidden places to relieve herself where her owners wouldn't see. Each time she was punished, her anxiety around going to the bathroom near her humans grew stronger. This fear only escalated the problem, creating a vicious cycle where Macie's behavior worsened, and her trust in her owners began to erode. What started as an isolated issue turned into a deeply ingrained problem driven by misunderstanding and fear.

Dogs live in the moment.

The only time you can correct a potty accident is if you catch the dog in the act and you respond in a calm manner <u>at the moment</u> the dog is pooping or peeing. If you come across an accident after the fact, you must ignore it.

Yes—ignore it, no matter how many times it happens.

If you take them to the spot where they peed 30 minutes ago they have absolutely no idea what you are punishing them for.

When I mention this to people, they often reply that a dog's sense of smell is so strong that they can detect the urine. And while that's true, they don't just smell the urine. They can also pick up on the carpet fibers, the spilled drink from days ago, the cleaning products you used, and even the treat they had earlier. So, how is the dog supposed to understand what they're being punished for? Why punish them at all if they were just playing with their ball when you brought them over? Was the ball the issue? It's not clear to the dog what they did wrong, and that confusion only makes the problem worse.

Your dog does not speak English, so you cannot verbally explain to the dog the reason he is being punished. Your actions will confuse the dog and the unwanted behavior will continue or escalate. The dog may even wonder why his humans are so unpredictable or come to the wrong conclusion. Or worse, the dog might lose his sense of safety and trust.

In Macie's case, she *did* realize she was being punished for peeing. What she did *not* understand was that it was *where* she was going that her owners were angry about. She thought: *my people do not want me to go pee.* This is an impossible request, of course, she simply must go pee. So her solution was to hide it and never pee in front of her humans.

Macie ended up having a UTI and got medication to clear it up, but it didn't fix what she learned from their punishment. Macie's owners had to reinforce all the original house training rules from when she was a puppy to get her over her fear. In other words, they had to start from scratch.

If you react to potty accidents with any fear tactics or pain methods, your dog may learn to distrust you. Once that bond is broken, it is difficult to rebuild.

When a dog does something, whether you view it as good

or bad, you only have a few seconds to either reinforce or discourage that behavior. Dog trainers will tell you that you only have 2-3 seconds to react to a behavior for the dog to make the desired connection. If you wait longer, your dog's mind is already on something else and you have lost the opportunity to intervene with that particular behavior.

But...there's good news!

Catching your puppy or new dog going to the bathroom in the house isn't the end of the world—it's actually a great opportunity to teach them! Sure, it might feel frustrating at first, but this is the perfect chance to guide your dog toward the right behavior. Instead of getting upset, think of it as a training moment.

If you catch your dog in the act, interrupt it with a firm "no" and, if possible, pick him up or guide him outside. Yes, you may end up with a little pee on you, but house training can be messy—that's just part of the process! The key is to show your dog what behavior is desirable, and nothing communicates that better than catching him mid-accident and showing him the right place to go. Once your dog finishes outside, make a huge deal out of it!

- Give him a treat
- Shower him with petting and positive attention
- Have a toy ready for a little playtime as a reward

The timing is everything. Be sure to reward him within seconds of him finishing his business outside so he connects the dots between going potty in the right place and getting praise.

Stay calm, act quickly, and your dog will start to understand what's expected. With patience, this phase will pass, and the accidents will happen less and less!

Let's Talk Leashes

When I brought Comet home at 8 weeks old, I was surprised to find out that I had to teach her how to walk on a leash. I had always assumed that all dogs just knew how to do it—after all, it seems like a pretty natural thing, right? But when we went for our first walk, Comet had no idea what to do. She just stood there, staring up at me like I was from another planet.

It's easy to expect our dogs to instinctively understand how to walk calmly beside us on a leash, but in reality, this concept is totally foreign to them—especially when you think about how dogs behave in the wild. Walking on a leash in a way that keeps the leash slack and curved is a learned skill. In loose leash walking, the goal is for you to be able to stroll down the street without being pulled or dragged along. And just like any skill, it takes practice.

If the only time you put your dog on a leash is the occasional walk or the trip to the vet, you cannot expect the dog to not pull. Actually, dogs will instinctively pull harder when the leash is tight. My huskies would love to treat me like a sled and pull me to whatever destination they see fit if I didn't teach them otherwise.

There are many ways to train your dog to walk loosely on a leash. Here are a few common ones:

1. Place a treat by his nose as he walks nicely by your side. Let him have the treat after a few steps and increase the distance between treats as he learns to walk calmly.

2. When he pulls, come to a complete stop or immediately change directions. His lack of progress will annoy him and he will soon learn that pulling is the action that is causing you to react in such a frustrating manner.
3. Change directions in a fun and engaging manner. Do this often and unexpectedly while putting a little pressure on the leash. This will train him to keep his focus on you and how to respond to leash pressure.

These are just a few quick tips but there are many methods and experienced trainers who can help you.

Leashes can be used…anywhere!

I am embarrassed to say I was well into my training journey before I learned that leashes can actually be used *anywhere* as a training tool. Even inside your house. What?! There are so many training reasons to have your dog leashed in your house.

When you have a puppy, leave them on a lightweight leash whenever he is not being crated. This way, if the puppy hides under the coach, you can gently pull them out or if they stick their nose somewhere it shouldn't be, you can guide them away from the trouble. I currently have a Siberian husky puppy. Her manners are improving everyday, but I still put a leash on her when my toddler-aged grandchildren comes to visit. This helps me control her if she gets too rambunctious and keeps her in my sight.

When learning basic commands, the leash is great for keeping your dog right where you want them. You can step on the leash to free up both your hands. On one hand you can keep a treat while giving hand signals with the other. The dog is free to move the length of the leash but cannot leave your training session.

You can use the leash to guide them when teaching them a new skill. For example, if you are teaching your dog to stay, start off with short distances. If the dog breaks his stay, it is a lot more constructive to have him on leash and guide him back to where you want them. The alternative is chasing him throughout the house which may quickly become a favorite game for your dog.

Crates

Crates have a reputation, but the reality is more nuanced. I remember when my neighbor got a golden retriever and frequently crated him. At the time, I thought it was cruel because I believed that a dog should be treated like family, and I didn't see the need for a crate. However, when used appropriately, a crate can actually provide a sense of security and comfort for your pet.

It's important to understand the distinction between misuse and proper use of a crate. When used correctly, a crate can become a safe haven, giving your dog a space to retreat, relax, and feel secure. My older dog loves her crate and has access to it 24/7, but I don't lock her in it. She goes in on her own to take peaceful naps, and I'm sure she thinks of it as her private dog bedroom.

There will inevitably be times when your dog will need to be crated, whether it's an overnight stay at the vet, boarding while you're on vacation, flying with your dog, or even a community emergency and evacuation. The crate should always be a safe space for your dog.

In fact, crate training is one of the best tools for house training.

Most dogs won't eliminate where they sleep, so if your dog can't be in your sight, they should be in the crate. It's that simple! You'll be amazed at how quickly your dog learns to potty outside when you follow this simple rule.

> *Tip: I remove my puppy's collar before placing her in the crate to prevent it from getting caught and causing a choking hazard if she tries to escape. Be sure to check that the crate is free of any potential hazards.*

If your dog is mature enough, you can try leaving them unsupervised and out of the crate. If the dog causes trouble, it's not the dog's fault—it's a sign that he wasn't ready for that level of freedom. Some dogs may never be suited for free reign when unsupervised, as each dog is unique. Freedom to roam the house is a privilege that must be earned. Until then, keep your dog in a crate when you're not able to supervise.

Is Your Dog Naughty or Just Bored?

Your home is likely one of your favorite places—it's filled with the people and things you love: books, clothes, electronics, and everything in between. Now, remember how it felt when we were housebound during the pandemic. Most of us went stir-crazy and longed for a change of scenery, even if it was just a quick trip to the grocery store. That's how most dogs feel every day.

You've probably heard the saying "a tired dog is a good dog," and while that's often true, I'd argue that a more accurate phrase would be "a bored dog is a destructive dog."

We often assume that if our dogs have a backyard, that's all they need. But that's simply not the case. Dogs crave adventure. They want new places to explore and new smells to discover. They need exercise—and for some breeds, that's essential for their well-being.

In fact, I'd say city dogs often lead more fulfilling lives than many suburban dogs. Why? Because if you live in an apartment without a backyard, you have no choice but to walk your dog every day—often multiple times. On the other hand, many suburban dogs spend the majority of their days never leaving their house or yard.

So, if you come home to a couch that's been chewed up, chances are your dog was just looking for something satisfying to do. It was bored and needed an outlet for its energy. Do you want that outlet to be a long walk, or your expensive area rug?

Finding a way to channel my dog's energy is what led me to dog sports. In Comet's first year, we took numerous obedience classes—everything from puppy training to advanced obedience. But even though she knew all her commands, she was still a bundle of energy and didn't fit the image I had of a well-mannered dog. She wasn't misbehaving, she was just so full of energy that I needed to find a way for her to release it without eating my cat or chewing up the legs of the kitchen table.

As dog owners, it's our responsibility to ensure our pets' needs are met. And that goes beyond just food and water. Dogs need exercise. They need playtime. They need opportunities to explore and enjoy new smells for a fulfilling, rewarding life.

Ideas to keep them busy:

- Take them on a long walk

- Explore new places together
- Go on a "sniff walk," where the goal is not distance, but letting your dog explore scents as long as they want
- Teach them a new trick
- Try a dog sport like agility, nose work, rally obedience, or barn hunt—these are great for keeping their brains engaged
- Do a breed-specific activity—retrievers love to retrieve, and snow dogs love to pull
- Feed them using puzzle feeders or make your own by rolling up their food in a towel
- Throw their food in the yard and let them "hunt" for it

Dogs need mental and physical stimulation. If you give them that, they'll be much less likely to turn your furniture into a chew toy!

Are You Training Your Dog or Just Confusing Him?

We often think we're training our dogs, but in reality, we might be confusing them instead. This book isn't a training manual, so I won't dive too deeply into the step-by-step details. However, I will highlight a few common mistakes we tend to make.

#1 Your Dog Does NOT Speak English

The phrase I repeat most often to my students is, "Your dog does not speak English." It's not just a catchy saying—it's the truth.

Yes, your dog likely knows words like sit, down, walk, treat, and a few others. But that's far from understanding the complexities of the English language. Let's break it down: you probably know a few words in languages you're not fluent in. For example, even if you don't speak Spanish, you likely understand words like *hola*, *adios*, *gracias*, and so on. But would that be enough to hold a conversation with a native speaker? If I spoke to you in Spanish, would you understand everything I said? Probably not. Knowing a few words doesn't equate to truly understanding the language.

That's why you can't expect your dog to understand a long-winded lecture about their behavior. It may sound funny, but I see it all the time—advanced rally obedience students verbally scolding their dogs. *All. The. Time.*

Now, don't get me wrong—I'm not saying you shouldn't talk to your dogs. I talk to mine all the time! Just keep in mind that they're more in tune with your body language and tone than the words themselves. When I praise them for good behavior, they hear the joy and pride in my voice. When I raise my voice to stop them from chasing each other in the house, they understand that I'm unhappy based on my tone.

Dogs don't naturally know how we want them to act. We need to teach them in ways they understand by rewarding the behaviors we want and discouraging the ones we don't. Verbal explanations won't get you far. Dogs understand praise—and they *definitely* understand treats and toys. By rewarding them in ways they recognize as positive, you'll soon see them acting in ways they know will please you.

#2 Timing is Key

Let's imagine I told you I'd give you $20 if you remembered my name. You say "Maria," but instead of immediately handing you the money and congratulating you, I get distracted, trying to recall where I put the $20 bill. If I take too long to acknowledge your correct answer, you'll start to think you were wrong. So, you say another name, "Margaret." Just as I remember that the $20 is in my back pocket, I hand it to you. What happens now? You'll likely call me "Margaret."

The big difference with humans is that we speak the same language. I can explain my mistake, and you'll know my name is Maria again. Your dog doesn't speak English, so an explanation will do nothing. With dogs, actions speak louder than words.

Let's use the "sit" command as an example. You tell your dog to sit, and it does. Great! But you fumble around with the treat for too long, and your dog stands up. Then you reward the dog with the treat. This entire process might take less than 10 seconds.

Does the dog understand what it's being rewarded for? Was it the sit? The stand? The combination of sit and stand? If left to the dog, it may think the reward is for any of those actions.

Rewards are often too slow or inconsistent, so it helps to use a word that clearly signals the positive behavior. This is called a "marker word." My marker word is "yes." It's simple, clear, and sounds positive—it's hard to make "yes" sound negative.

When teaching your dog to sit, say "yes!" as soon as their butt touches the floor, then immediately reward them with a treat. The marker word, given at the right time, buys you a moment to deliver the treat. The dog will quickly learn to work for the "yes."

There are two more benefits to using a marker word. First, we don't always have training treats on hand, but we almost always have words. Second, you won't always need treats. Once the dog has learned the commands, you can phase out treats except for occasional rewards. We don't want our dogs to listen only when they think a treat is coming. A marker word will always encourage good behavior without the need for constant treats.

#3 Be Consistently Consistent

Consistency with dogs means doing things the same way *and* using the same words every time you do the same action. It is vital that everyone in the household is on the same page with the dog's training in order for the dog to truly grasp the behavior you want. Make sure everyone in the household follows the same protocol by using the same words. Those words should only have one meaning for the dog if you want the dog to have a clear understanding of the command. Our use of the word "down" is probably the most common error when it comes to the words we use with our dogs.

I have trained my dog to respond to the word "down" by lying down with all her elbows and tummy touching the ground. One day, I entered the living room and my dog was laying on the couch. My husband told my dog to "get down." Comet didn't budge. Actually, she looked content. She was in a perfect down position, just like Dad told her to. *I'm such a good girl!*

My husband started to get frustrated. His tone changed, and his body language indicated he was unhappy with her. But why? She was doing exactly what he had asked. Fortunately, I stepped in before he accidentally undid all my training with the word "down." In this case, my husband used a command my dog knew but attached a different meaning to the word. The dog doesn't understand that a human word could have multiple meanings. Since then, we've adopted the command "move" for when she's sitting in his spot.

Let's look at another example.

Your friend comes over to visit, and your overexcited dog jumps all over them. Your first reaction is to tell your dog to get down. Your dog knows the word "down," so he immediately plops to the floor. In this case, the "down" command did achieve the desired outcome, but we want to make things as clear as possible for your dog. By using a different command, like "off," it's easier for him to understand exactly what you want. "Off" means "don't jump on that person," but he can still be sitting, lying down, or standing. "Down" has only one meaning: a lying down position.

What about when your front door is open? It's crucial to train your dog that an open door doesn't mean it's time for him to bolt outside, get lost, or run into traffic. Teach your dog to wait for your permission to go outside every time—whether it's the front door or the back door leading to the yard. After all, the gate might be ajar, or an animal could be outside. If there's a behavior you want your dog to consistently follow, you need to not only teach it, but also reinforce it regularly.

Consistency across your household is key. If each person uses different words for the same command, your dog won't understand that "stay" and "don't move" mean the same thing.

I saw this play out perfectly with a family in my youth dog training club. They were struggling with recall (the "come" command)—or, more specifically, the husband was. He said, "The dog just doesn't like me." When the wife and kids called the dog, he always came, but when it was the husband's turn, the dog ignored him. I asked them to demonstrate. The wife and kids went to different corners of the training area, each calling the dog with "Rocky, come" or just "come," and Rocky happily trotted over. When it was Dad's turn, he called, "Get over here, buddy." Rocky glanced at him but kept ignoring him. The husband turned to me and said, "See what I mean?"

The problem was clear, but it wasn't so obvious to the family. When I explained the issue, the husband argued that it all meant the same thing. But to the dog, "Get over here, buddy" was as meaningless as "paper orange turn desk." It was just a jumble of words.

You can choose any word you want for your dog's commands, but everyone must use the same word consistently. "Stay" means "stay" because that's the meaning we've given it. You could even teach your dog to stay with the word "triangle," as long as everyone in your household is consistent in using that word.

A word of caution: don't get too fancy or personalized with your commands. While it's fun to see people use foreign languages in competitions—like when a German Shepherd handler uses German phrases—it's a good idea to choose words that anyone can understand. After all, if my dogs are with someone other than me, I want them to follow commands in a language that makes sense to their temporary human. Not everyone knows German.

Is Your Dog Being a Jerk or Is He Just Confused?

I often hear people say their dogs are jerks (or use far more colorful adjectives). They tell me the dog will only listen at certain times, with certain people, or in specific situations. But is the dog actually being a jerk, or is it just confused?

I'm not saying your dog never acts like a jerk. My little angels certainly have their moments. Dogs are thinking, feeling beings, and sometimes they just want to be left alone. That's not what I'm talking about here. But if your dog only listens in certain situations or with certain people, it likely means they either don't understand the command or you've accidentally taught them the wrong thing.

I've had people tell me their dog ignores them at first and only listens on the third command. They assume the dog is being willful, but what's likely happening is that you've unknowingly taught your dog that the word "sit" doesn't really mean anything. What you may have taught them is that the phrase "sit sit SIT" should be followed by action.

Sometimes people tell me their dog only listens to the "sit" command when they're holding a treat in front of the dog's face. Does the dog actually know what "sit" means? It's possible that the word "sit" has no meaning to the dog at all. You may have taught them that the hand gesture in front of their face is the cue for sitting, not the word "sit" itself.

Dogs are experts at reading our body language, and sometimes we accidentally send the wrong signals. They've evolved to pick up on even the smallest cues. For example, when I run agility with my dog, the tiniest movement will tell her which obstacle to take next. If she's on my left and I lift my shoulder, she knows to turn right. If my shoulder drops, she turns left. An experienced agility dog might take the wrong obstacle simply because the handler shifted their body—whether it's a shoulder, hip, or arm—just a fraction of a second the wrong way while running full speed. Our dogs are so tuned into us that it only takes an instant for them to receive the wrong information.

If your dog only listens at certain times, try to notice any patterns. What are you doing when they listen versus when they don't? Are you always standing in the same position? Does your dog listen inside the house but not outside? Only in the living room, but not anywhere else in the house?

It's not uncommon for someone to think their dog knows a command when they don't. Even those of us who should know better can fall into this trap.

When I competed in obedience and rally obedience with Comet, my instructor—a respected AKC judge—said he didn't think Comet knew the heel command. What? Of course, she did! She just wasn't enthusiastic and sometimes lagged behind. By that point, I had been taking obedience classes for years, and Comet had competed in the master class of rally obedience— the highest of its five competition classes. Of course, she knew what "heel" meant! But he suggested I take a specific class to address the lagging issue, and I respected his opinion, thinking it couldn't hurt.

Guess what? Comet didn't know the heel command.

Heeling isn't just about movement; it's about position. Specifically, it's when your dog is on your left side, with their shoulders lined up to your hip. The dog doesn't have to be moving to be in the correct heel position. They could be sitting. But Comet had interpreted the "heel" command to mean that she should walk alongside me. And alongside, to her, could mean beside me, in front of me, or behind me. Since she usually did it correctly, I hadn't realized there was a miscommunication.

Our dogs aren't usually being jerks. If you're having a training issue, stop and examine what's actually happening. Where is the problem occurring? Have someone record your interactions and review them. Is your body language sending mixed cues? Or are you giving the wrong cue altogether? Does your dog truly understand what's being asked of them?

Bad Habits We Unintentionally Reinforce

Your dog is always learning. Every day, we are either teaching him something new or reinforcing a behavior the dog already knows. These behaviors can be something positive, such as leaving unattended human food alone or negative, such as counter surfing for scraps of unattended food. The way we react to everyday situations teaches them what is encouraged and what we are willing to tolerate.

We are often our worst enemy when it comes to dog training. Sometimes our dog's most annoying habits are unknowingly being reinforced by us. Most of the time we chalk these habits up to an irritating dog rather than seeing our part in the problem.

A coworker asked me my opinion on how to solve an ongoing issue with her 10-year-old Yorkshire terrier. The dog was not allowed in the upstairs portion of their house where the bedrooms are located. She then detailed the nightly ritual that goes on in her house.

Every night, when the family went to bed the dog remained on the first floor by way of a gate at the bottom of the stairs. The dog whined and barked nonstop to show her displeasure about being left downstairs while her family members were all snuggled upstairs in their comfy beds. The family tried to ignore her. Eventually, they yelled at her with no positive results. After about 30 minutes, someone got frustrated enough with the noise and went to get the dog who then joined one of them in bed. This nightly ritual went on for 10 years! My coworker really thought they had a "no dogs in the bedrooms" rule but what they actually had was a "dog is allowed upstairs but only after a nightly entrance fee" rule. They taught the dog that 30 minutes of whining and barking was required to get an invitation upstairs, and reinforced it by caving in night after night for years.

Every interaction we have with our dogs is a learning moment. If you never feed your dog from the dinner table, he won't learn to beg for food there. By 'never,' I mean not even once. If he never encounters the opportunity to get a tasty piece of roast from the table, he won't think it's an option. However, once he's experienced it, he won't forget. Your actions directly influence your dog's behavior.

You might think giving him an occasional scrap of meat is harmless, but this can lead to unwanted behavior. For instance, if your dog starts whining for table scraps, will you still see it as a minor issue when he won't leave your dinner guests alone on Thanksgiving? Your actions have taught him that the dinner table is a place to get treats, even if you didn't mean for it to be that way.

Dogs perceive things simply: something is either allowed or it isn't. Decide on the behaviors you want and consistently model them. Your dog is constantly observing your actions and reactions to learn how to navigate the human world.

4

Feeding Your Furry Friend

Feeding your dog isn't just about the food you choose; it's also about how you approach mealtime. The way you feed your dog can have a significant impact on their behavior, manners, and overall relationship with food. From establishing routines to encouraging patience and discouraging begging, the process of feeding is an opportunity for training and reinforcing positive behaviors.

Food – The Great Motivator

We all feed our dogs at least once a day, often without considering what a powerful tool we're overlooking when we simply set the food bowl down and walk away.

While our dogs may not always know exactly what we want from them, they all know one thing: they must eat. Eating is essential to life, and it's especially motivating for pups. Beyond meals and the occasional training treat, you can turn food and feeding times into one of your strongest allies when training your dog.

For the first month after my puppy joined our family, she didn't eat from a bowl. I measured how much food she needed each day and fed her by hand. I kept her food in a treat pouch that I wore all day long, wanting her to realize that her food came from me, not from the bowl on the floor. Just seeing me place the bowl down wasn't enough. I wanted her to have no doubt that I controlled the food.

At first, I gave her small portions every time she made eye contact with me. I then added a small handful when she responded to her name. Eventually, I moved on to simple commands. She didn't eat from a bowl until about two months later.

What did this accomplish?

I got a dog who knew she had to rely on me for the basics of life. Doing what I asked and being well-behaved earned her what she wanted most—food. From her point of view, being well-behaved was beneficial to her.

I also got a dog who learned to take food from a human's hand gently. If she was too wild when taking food, the feeding simply stopped. No yelling or fussing—I'd just put the food back in the pouch until another opportunity arose. She learned this quickly.

When I did eventually graduate to a bowl, I always paired a command she knew with feeding time. I'd ask her to sit, down, or stay in place before placing the bowl down.

I chose to hand-feed for two months, but there's no magic number. Some people hand-feed throughout their dog's life. You can hand-feed for as long or as short a time as you feel is beneficial! Every dog and household is different, after all.

Free Feeding vs Scheduled Feeding

Beyond hand-feeding, there are two feeding methods that are almost universally practiced: free feeding and scheduled feeding.

- **Free feeding** is when a full bowl of dog food is placed down on the floor and refilled or replaced when the bowl is empty.
- **Scheduled feeding** is when your dog is fed at certain predetermined intervals throughout the day.

Think of the difference between these two methods as the contrast between a 24-hour all-you-can-eat buffet and having breakfast, lunch, and dinner at consistent times each day. No veterinarian or dog trainer I know recommends free feeding; in fact, it's strongly discouraged. I understand that we're all busy, and it can be tempting to simply put down a bowl and forget about it. With automatic feeders, it can seem even easier to simplify our hectic lives. But why complicate things by creating potential problems down the road?

When you free-feed, there's no way to monitor exactly how much your dog is eating. This becomes especially problematic if you have multiple dogs sharing the same bowl, as it's nearly impossible to track individual food intake. Without a structured feeding schedule, your dog may develop stomach issues that go unnoticed. Dogs can't verbally communicate discomfort, so if one starts experiencing gastrointestinal problems or loses their appetite, you might not realize something is wrong until the issue has escalated to noticeable weight loss or other serious symptoms.

The opposite is also true. Your dog could end up gaining an

unhealthy amount of weight by eating to its heart's content every day. In homes with more than one dog, free feeding can create a serious problem. One dog might start seeing the food bowl as a prized possession and decide it's all his. If you're at work while this is happening, you won't be able to step in. When a dog gets possessive like this, he might view the other dog—or even a child who comes too close to the bowl—as a threat. Resource guarding is a serious issue that can lead to nasty dog fights or even attacks. If this problem arises, it's crucial to get help from a trained professional immediately.

When you free-feed, you are also giving away your most powerful training tool. You don't want your dog to ever think his food comes from a magical, refilling bowl that is always available to him. You want there to be no doubt in his mind that his meals are supplied by you.

Scheduled feeding is the way to go. A hungry dog is motivated to work for food. Now, I'm not suggesting you keep your dog hungry all the time, but rather that you incorporate feeding into your training routine. Before placing down the bowl, ask your dog to perform a behavior they know well. Don't always ask for a sit—mix it up and get creative. You might ask for a stay, then place the bowl on the other side of the room and release your dog. If your dog breaks the stay, don't put the bowl down until they get it right. They'll still get to eat, but if they're being stubborn, it might take a little longer—maybe ten minutes instead of two.

If your dog is not hungry and ignores the bowl, pick it up in about 10 minutes. Feeding time is now over until the next meal. A routine will also allow you to observe any changes in your dog's eating habits early on, helping you catch potential health concerns before they become severe.

Taking Food from Your Dog

A popular training exercise many people try involves taking food from the dog while he's eating. Typically, this is done by placing something tempting, like a dog treat, on top of the food in the bowl, then reaching in and taking it away with your hand. In theory, this is done to teach the dog to allow you to take food away without any issues.

I can't honestly say if this works or not. I have never done this myself. To me, it seems like it would be counterproductive. I do the exact opposite and have had great results.

Rather than taking food away, I add yummy morsels at random and unpredictable times. I may throw a small piece of ham or chicken on top of the bowl mid-meal. My dogs never know when this manna from heaven will appear. What they *do* know is that a human hand near their bowl can be a great thing and don't feel the need to guard their bowl.

I also do this occasionally when they have something of mediocre interest. In other words, I always trade up. A piece of chicken is more valuable to my dog than a stick, a piece of cheese may be more valuable than an old toy. Let's say they are chewing on a stick in the yard and I ask them to relinquish it in exchange for a piece of chicken or a new toy. I want them to know that it is their best interest to listen to me. They will be rewarded and they know it.

These training exercises, along with the 'leave it' and 'drop it' commands commonly taught in beginner obedience or puppy classes, have ensured that my dogs never develop issues with guarding or stealing food.

5

Tall Tails: Myths About Dogs & Their Behavior

As much as we love our dogs and consider them part of the family, the truth is that we often misunderstand them. Dogs communicate in ways that are very different from humans, and what seems like straightforward behavior to us might have an entirely different meaning in the canine world. These misunderstandings can lead to frustration, confusion, and sometimes even strained relationships between us and our furry friends. In this chapter, we'll bust common myths and explore the realities of dog behavior. By understanding the truth, we can better appreciate our dogs for who they truly are.

Your Dog Is Not a Racist

Dogs are incredible creatures, full of love, loyalty, and an endless capacity for connection. Yet, despite all their wonderful qualities, one of the most persistent myths about dogs is that they can be prejudiced like humans.

I've heard people say:

- My dog doesn't like people of a certain sex.
- My dog doesn't like people of a certain race.
- My dog doesn't like people in a particular profession.
- My rescue dog must have been abused by _____ because he doesn't like _____.

But dogs don't see the world through the same lens we do. They don't judge others based on appearance, race, or background. Instead, a dog's behavior is shaped by their experiences, training, and the environment around them. In most cases, what might seem like prejudice is often due to lack of proper socialization. While some dogs may have a legitimate fear based on a past negative experience, more often than not, it's simply fear of the unknown.

Like most animals, dogs have evolved to instinctively fear what is strange or unfamiliar. This natural wariness helped keep wild animals safe, and domestic dogs still retain this trait. Puppies, in particular, have a critical socialization window during which they should be exposed to as many different people, places, and things as possible before the age of six months. The earlier, the better. For instance, a three-month-old puppy that frequently encounters people in uniforms will not see a firefighter as a threat.

A four-year-old Cocker Spaniel named Cally is a strong example of a dog who was never properly socialized. Cally spent the first three years of her life in a crate with limited interaction, only seeing adult women who were all white. When she was surrendered and adopted by a new family, she was extremely fearful. She was scared of people, especially men and children, and terrified of most other dogs unless they were smaller than her. Cally had been traumatized, but fortunately, her new family understood her needs and worked with a qualified behaviorist. Over time and with a lot of patience, Cally's panic subsided, though she remains a work in progress.

Many people mistakenly think that socialization simply means allowing a dog to interact with as many dogs as possible. But true socialization is about getting a dog comfortable in the presence of other dogs, without necessarily interacting with them. It's important to expose your dog to situations where other dogs are present while rewarding calm behavior. For example, reward your dog when they focus on you instead of reacting to other dogs. A dog that becomes agitated when seeing another dog on a walk likely hasn't been properly socialized.

Take my older dog, for example. Walking with her is a peaceful, enjoyable experience—exactly what most people envision when they think of walking their dog. My 7-month-old puppy, on the other hand, is still learning. She's extremely friendly and thinks every dog and person she meets is a potential playmate. A squirrel in the distance? She'll try to chase it without a second thought, even if it means pulling me off my feet.

Friendly dogs are not necessarily well-socialized dogs.

Is your dog able to calmly stay at your side when encountering other dogs? Does he remain composed when a bike passes by or when seeing someone in a wheelchair? Does the sight of a hat make him react?

At one competition, I witnessed a judge with a large, flowing tie. About a quarter of the dogs were fearful of the tie and shied away from the judge. These dogs had been trained for obedience exams, yet they were afraid of something unfamiliar. This illustrates how a dog's fear can be triggered by new, unfamiliar experiences. The more exposure a dog has to different people, objects, and situations, the more confident and accepting they will become. An insecure dog that hasn't been well-socialized is more likely to react with fear, and sometimes aggression.

It's never too late to socialize your dog. Older dogs may require more time and patience, but the process can still be effective. If your dog experiences severe anxiety, it's important to seek help from a trained behaviorist.

To socialize your dog, you must expose them to a variety of experiences in a calm and controlled manner. Don't rush the process. For instance, don't throw your dog into the chaos of a busy park and expect them to remain calm. Instead, gradually introduce them to the situation. Start by walking across the street from the park, then sit on the grass at the far end while your dog observes the children playing. Over time, reduce the distance and reward your dog for calmly watching the scene. Eventually, you can confidently walk through the park without your dog becoming agitated.

You can begin socializing your dog right away by exposing them to different people, places, sounds, animals, textures, and surfaces. Consider exposing your dog to a variety of people: individuals of different ages, sizes, races, and abilities. For example, introduce them to people riding bikes, running, dancing, or carrying large bags. Expose them to people who use medical equipment, like wheelchairs, oxygen masks, walkers, or crutches—especially if you want to eventually become a therapy dog team.

Some dogs may even show fear of other dogs based on their appearance or breed. I've had many people tell me that their otherwise friendly dog dislikes certain colors or breeds. The solution is to expose them to a variety of dogs in a safe and calm manner. The goal is not to make your dog interact with every dog they meet but to teach them to remain calm and composed around other dogs.

A well-socialized dog is one who can walk past another dog without feeling the urge to engage. It's not about forcing interactions but about fostering calm and confidence in a variety of situations.

Teaching an Older Dog New Tricks

Our canine friends are unfortunately the victims of ageism. Older dogs are usually overlooked at shelters. Many selfish people will rehome or surrender their old dogs to a shelter once they start to become sick or less playful. Often these unscrupulous people will replace the old dog with a puppy. In my opinion this is a sin of the greatest order.

I'm not getting down on people that have a legitimate reason to rehome a pet. There are times when rehoming a dog is the correct choice. If the owner is no longer able to care for the dog, if the new baby is allergic to the dog, or if the dog is truly aggressive and his needs are more than you can handle, it makes sense to find that dog a more suitable home than yours. That is not what I am talking about. I am referring to the people that unload the dog just because he is no longer that fun, active, cute ball of fur.

And then we come to that old myth – *You can't teach an old dog new tricks.*

This little nugget is false and does a great disservice to our older dogs. You can definitely teach a dog something new at any point in his life. But I will add that you have to be realistic about what you want to teach your older dog.

An older dog may take more time and patience, but he will catch on to new skills. If you are rescuing an older dog from a shelter, his previous household may never have trained him at all or he may have been a stray. This dog may have never been asked to perform basic commands. He may have never stepped into a training facility. You may be starting from scratch. This is when patience is worth its weight in gold. Your dog will come to understand what you want from it, but it could take a little longer than a puppy. My son adopted two adult dogs of different breeds. One of them learned commands eagerly, while the other still struggles. Both, however, were easily house trained. A puppy comes with puppy-specific issues like an immature bladder and teething, so if you're going to get a dog, know that there will always be challenges.

You have to be realistic when you decide what to teach an older dog. You must consider his age, activity level, and any physical limits he may have. Basic commands can be taught at any age. Basic tricks such as spins and high fives can be taught at any age. There is a world of dog sports and dog friendly activities that you can also teach an older dog. Yes, your older dog can learn anything that a young dog can learn. They have the same mental abilities. But just because you can doesn't always mean you should.

I currently have two Siberian huskies, one is 12-years-old and the other is a puppy. These are two very different dogs. While Huskies were bred to pull sleds, my older dog has never done this, so there's no way I would expect her to take on such a physically demanding activity at her age. On the other hand, my puppy is strong and energetic enough to start learning the ropes of sled pulling, so I'm introducing her to it now, and I have the time to teach her.

My older dog has been involved in agility since she was one year old, but a few years ago, I realized it was time for her to stop. She began hesitating at the jumps and struggled with tasks like judging the width of the dog walk. I suspected that her joints might be hurting, and her eyesight could be declining, so we decided to stop agility. Instead, I turned to a new dog sport that doesn't require as much physical exertion: scent work.

Scent work is perfect for older dogs because it taps into something they naturally love—sniffing—and turns it into a fun game! In this sport, the dog is trained to find specific scents, like birch or cypress. They then search an area for the hidden scent and communicate the location of the "hide" to the handler. The handler doesn't know where the hide is, so they must learn to read the dog's signals to pinpoint the location.

Barn Hunt is another great option that's similar to scent work, but with a twist: the dog searches for rats. Don't worry—these are healthy, well-cared-for rats, safely contained in a protected environment. The rats are usually hidden in places where the dog can smell them but can't reach them, such as in a stack of hay.

Both of these activities are perfect for older dogs because they don't require any strenuous physical activity. There's no jumping, so they don't put pressure on the dog's joints, and it keeps their mind sharp while letting them engage in something they naturally enjoy.

Can Dogs See Colors?

One of the most common myths is that dogs see in black and white. This isn't true; however, their color perception is quite different from ours. Dogs have fewer cones in their eyes, which limits their ability to see the full spectrum of colors that humans can. A more accurate comparison would be to someone with red-green color blindness.

You might have noticed that your dog's favorite toy is blue, or perhaps purple. Blue stands out most to them, with purple coming in second. While they can distinguish between different shades of yellow and gray, their perception of red and green is far from what we experience. Instead, dogs see the world in shades of brown, yellow, and gray, with pops of blue and purple.

This difference in color vision is important to keep in mind when choosing toys and training accessories for your dog. A green ball, for example, might be hard to find in a patch of green grass, but a blue ball will stand out more easily. Making their toys easier to spot can enhance their enjoyment and engagement.

6

It all starts with you

A happy, well-trained dog is truly a blessing—the heart of your family. Too often, myths and misconceptions can stand in the way of what we should be doing to nurture a positive relationship with our pets. But the good news is, it's never too late to get on the right track.

If you don't train them, you can't blame them.

This simple motto is one I've heard in nearly every training facility I know, and it's spot on. As dog owners, it's our responsibility to teach our dogs what's expected of them. Training isn't just about teaching commands—it's about building trust, understanding, and a lasting bond between you and your dog.

If you're experiencing challenges with your dog's behavior, it's important to reach out to a trained and qualified trainer or animal behaviorist. Professional guidance can make all the difference in addressing any issues.

If your dog shows signs of aggression or resource guarding, don't wait. These behaviors can escalate and become dangerous if left unchecked. A qualified professional is crucial to navigating these situations safely and effectively. Please seek help if needed.

I hope that my experiences and insights have helped shed light on the best ways to live harmoniously with your canine companions. Remember, I started out as someone who knew very little—my dog knowledge came mostly from TV, movies, and experiences with other people's dogs. I had no special talent other than recognizing when I was in over my head and seeking out the help I needed. My biggest asset was not giving up.

Now, it's your turn. You have the tools, the knowledge, and the power to build a stronger bond with your dog. Keep learning, keep training, and most importantly, enjoy the journey. Your dog's happiness and well-being depend on you—and there's no better time than now to get started.

www.ingramcontent.com/pod-product-compliance
Lightning Source LLC
Chambersburg PA
CBHW070107100426
42743CB00012B/2672